Jiha Moon

This publication accompanies the exhibition

Jiha Moon:
Double Welcome, Most Everyone's Mad Here
Co-curated by Mark Sloan & Amy Moorefield

The Halsey Institute of Contemporary Art at the College of Charleston produced this catalogue in association with the Taubman Museum of Art in Roanoke, Virginia.

Editor: Mark Sloan of the Halsey Institute of Contemporary Art
Associate Editors: Lori Kornegay, Bryan Granger, and Katie McCampbell
Photography: Rick Rhodes
Graphic Designer: Mark Lawrence of Gil Shuler Graphic Design
Copy Editor: Harriet Whelchel

TRAVELING ITINERARY

Taubman Museum of Art
Roanoke, VA
May 2 – September 20, 2015

Halsey Institute of Contemporary Art
College of Charleston
Charleston, SC
October 24 – December 5, 2015

Kalamazoo Institute of Arts
Kalamazoo, MI
December 19, 2015 – March 6, 2016

Salina Art Center
Salina, KS
April 6 – June 12, 2016

Jule Collins Smith Museum of Fine Art
Auburn University
Auburn, AL
January 21 – April 30, 2017

Richard E. Peeler Art Center
DePauw University
Greencastle, IN
August 25 – October 29, 2017

Tarble Arts Center
Eastern Illinois University
Charleston, IL
November 18, 2017 – February 4, 2018

American University Art Museum
American University
Washington, DC
March 31 – May 20, 2018

Jiha Moon
Double Welcome, Most Everyone's Mad Here

With essays by **Amy Moorefield & Lilly Wei**
And an interview with the artist by **Rachel Reese**
Edited by **Mark Sloan**

CONTENTS:

Jiha Moon:
Double Welcome,
Most Everyone's Mad Here

Jiha Moon harvests cultural elements native to Korea, Japan, and China and then unites them with Western elements to investigate the multifaceted nature of our current global identity as influenced by popular culture, technology, racial perceptions, and folklore. In more than fifty compositions that appear both familiar and foreign simultaneously, the artist blurs the lines between Western- and Eastern-identified iconography, depicting, for example, smartphone emojis and characters from the online game *Angry Birds* floating alongside Asian tigers and Indian gods.

Moon's witty and ironic art explores how Westerners perceive other cultures and how people in those other cultures in turn perceive the West. Korean born, now living in Atlanta, Georgia, Moon asks the pertinent question, "Why do people love foreign stuff so much? When we travel to other countries, explore different cultures, and meet with new people, we tend to fall in love with things that are not our own. People have a soft spot for foreign things. The world is so interconnected nowadays, how can you even tell where someone or something 'comes from' anymore?" In her work, Moon acts in the role of a traveler, exploring the notion that identity is not beholden to geographic location.

Honoring traditional Asian arts through her use of Hanji, Korean silk, and calligraphic brushstrokes, she plays with iconography and symbols that have been classified as "foreign," such as blue willow china patterns (developed in England, inspired by Chinese export ware), fortune cookies (which originated in California but are identified as Chinese), Korean fans, and floating dragons, and intermingles them with references to pop art and Southern folk art.

Her use of the peach, identified in Chinese mythology as a symbol of immortality, is also in homage to to her adopted state of Georgia, whose signature fruit is the peach. Moon transforms a traditional Korean fashion accessory called *norigae* into endearing quirky manifestations of various personalities with names like Gloria and Rachel whose hair is interwoven with eclectic items such as children's plastic barrettes or Native American beaded dolls. Her misshapen and whimsical ceramics reference Southern folk art face jugs yet are made using traditional Asian ceramic glazes and motifs. At the heart of this recent body of work, Moon presents an installation featuring stereotypical elements of Asian home decor: low wooden tables and embroidered silk pillows placed on Japanese tatami mats. Displayed on the various surfaces are her unconventional ceramic works, reflecting her interest in the "beautiful awkward," her description of tourists' desire to collect foreign and exotic elements to beautify their houses back home.

At first glance, Jiha Moon's work appears as a mash-up of high- and lowbrow cultural allusions. Upon further inspection, slyly ironic and humorous references satirically filtered by the artist become evident, reminding us that our preconceived notion of "others" is not a true manifestation of actual identity.

Amy Moorefield
Deputy Director of Exhibitions and Collections,
Taubman Museum of Art, Roanoke, Virginia

Moonstruck in Wonderland
Lilly Wei

Jiha Moon is not a theorist, not an ideologue, not a placard-waving agitator for social justice. She is not particularly invested in notions of "orientalism" as so brilliantly discussed by the late Palestinian-American cultural critic and theorist Edward Said in two of his most influential books, *Orientalism* (1978) and *Culture and Imperialism* (1993). Since then, our thinking has evolved (or so we would like to believe), becoming more informed, more nuanced, more sensitized, in large part due to his insights. Difference is now swirled with the familiar as the world becomes smaller, as common concerns bind us and our common humanity seeps through, beyond stereotypes and the superficialities and inanities of commercialized tourism and global capitalism. There is an international culture that is instantaneously accessible to countless millions of people via the Internet and social media, technology bringing all of us closer together, blurring boundaries, for better and worse. As for the ever increasing numbers of travelers who circle the globe regularly (and they are not only the one percent), to be elsewhere on some levels is very much like being here (even beyond the worldwide ubiquity of certain American and European brands, American pop culture, and English as the world's unofficial official language) where what used to be far-flung is seldom less than twenty-four hours away.

That said, our sense of the "other" has also become more fraught—who here was not deeply jolted by the attack on the World Trade Center, when the unthinkable occurred and the United States mainland itself was violated? As the world seems to be erupting uncontrollably into pervasive zones of irreconcilable conflict, we have exchanged our former, often blissfully naïve, Disneyfied notions of other cultures for one that is much darker, albeit no less stereotyped and reductive. The other, no longer exotic, erotic, and feminized, there for our pleasurable consumption, is now the enemy, the terrorist, to be distrusted, feared, hated. Over there is

no longer so far away; over there is here.

Moon's work is more about the social than politics, but inevitably, it backs into the latter. Navigating cultures and chronologies, trawling for images from which she creates "portmanteau" objects (a term coined by Lewis Carroll in *Through the Looking Glass* to describe the merging of two or more existing words to form a new word), she asks her viewers to consider the complexity of cultural heritage and identity, and how malleable they can be. Born and raised in Daegu, Korea, Moon studied art at Korea University in Seoul, earned her M.F.A. from the University of Iowa in Iowa City, and now lives in Atlanta, her work reflecting her own responses as a bemused stranger, at least at first. And her observations of another culture (Iowa and the South might seem foreign to a New Yorker, let alone a young woman from Korea) are all the more perceptive because of it. However—and understandably—she insists that her artwork should not be categorized as merely an East-West comparison, itself a cliché by now. What Moon offers us is more current, more absurdist and absorptive, more humorous and tongue-in-cheek, as she investigates aspects of influence, authorship, originality, appropriation, and identity. "While it might look Asian," she said, "it is all about America."

Double Welcome, Most Everyone's Mad Here is the title of Moon's lively and endearing exhibition of mischievously plundered, reconfigured images made in an array of media and materials. The title is taken from Lewis Carroll's beloved *Alice's Adventures in Wonderland*, filtered through the globally distributed 1951 animated Disney film, indeed, a double greeting from an erudite Oxford don's satire masquerading as a children's tale and a Hollywood mogul's pop entertainment. In the film, Alice, searching for the White Rabbit, encounters the Cheshire Cat. When she asks him for directions, he directs her to the Mad Hatter, and when Alice objects, he introduces her to the March Hare, who, he says, is also mad. He nonchalantly adds, "Most every-one's mad here," concluding, as he begins to disappear, "I'm not all there myself."

In a tribute to both Carroll and Disney, Moon makes her own Wonderland, her own Looking Glass world, where meanings are doubled, tripled, inverted, subverted, and in flux, her clever, extravagant exhibition spurred by her own affinity for sense and nonsense. Cannily and exhaustively collecting images as they capture her fancy, she tosses them together as if into a cross-pollinated cultural bouilla-baisse, calibrating their interaction, watching them simmer and transform. What she does so well is to take the ac-customed and extract something fresh from it, something unexpected, often strange. Upending formal hierarchies, she allows multiple genres—ink drawing, collage, painting, etching, woodblock printing, cyanotype, ceramics, embroi-dery, graphic design, fashion, screen prints, and more, using both figuration and abstraction—to co-exist, jostling each other. She jumbles together fine arts, pop art, design, fash-ion, advertisements, text, and Internet icons for the viewer to happily puzzle over and revel in.

Moon often uses Korean Hanji, an elegant mulberry paper (paper has long been the preferred support of traditional Asian painting and calligraphy and increasingly used by American and European artists). She then very consciously applies modern acrylic paint to Hanji, explain-ing that she likes to mix old and new together, her brush-work boldly gestural and exquisitely precise, a dexterity learned from calligraphic studies. Fabric, such as tie-dye, or resist-dye cotton or silk (like Hanji, they are materials associated with the East) often appears in her projects. The brightly colored textiles banding some of her paintings and wall pieces suggest a classic Western frame as well as an elaborately bordered Korean bedspread, a traditional wed-ding gift. They might also suggest other bedclothes such as quilts, the handiwork of accomplished, too often anony-mous women, such as the fine quilt makers of the American South. Shoelaces, doilies, glitter, beads, rhinestones, gold leaf—all craft materials—turn up regularly in her creations.

She reinterprets traditional Korean accessories such as *norigae*, a good-luck charm typically worn suspended from a woman's robes. Attached by a ring or loop, its central ornament might be a jewel, a heavy silk tassel swinging from it. Moon replaces the *norigae*'s gem with, for instance, a ceramic component that conjures up a mask or a peach or both, claiming kinship with the painted, embellished *kachinas* of Native Americans from the Southwest as well as other ritual objects and folk toys from a spectrum of cultures. Adding different types of hair to replace the

tassels, she reminds us about our crowning glory's vexed social and racial status. A complicated subject, hair is a distinctive physical trait that can be synonymous with difference, evoking shame as well as defiance and fierce pride.

The motifs that Moon incorporate are deceptive, ambiguous. She doesn't want them to be identified easily—or identified at all—the slippage between object and meaning a space that offers the imagination room to ramble about. She wants to "shake things up," she said, and "misunderstandings" are crucial toward understanding, including her own. Her sources are equally unclear; some motifs that look Asian might not be, and the reverse. Possibly the clouds drifting across the surface of some of the paintings are from Buddhist paintings, but they might also be Baroque. Tang dynasty landscapes might also be European surrealist fantasies or from Mexican folk art. Chinese fortune cookies, unknown in China, originated in California. Moon's very appealing replicas are produced in glossy, painted ceramic, at times decorated with Picasso-like faces, animals—she has a menagerie of invented creatures at her disposal—and little red, green, and black squares and dots.

Her marvelously variegated ceramics—she likes to join the ungainly with the graceful, the grotesque with the comely—might have been inspired by ancient Native American and Asian vessels or the popular face jars of Southern folk art and *Angry Birds*, from the popular children's game. Some depict misshapen faces that suggest ogres in meltdown, masks from traditional Asian theater or transmogrified portraits of actors from *ukiyo-e* prints, seen also in her paintings, and some are more Western, with big, long-lashed eyes, and slightly menacing, Chiclet-toothed smiles like that of the Cheshire Cat, mass-produced kitschy souvenirs turned into the one-off.

Other metamorphoses include blending distinctive Pennsylvania Dutch imagery, such as stylized birds with Korean phoenixes, and Twitter Birds. Blue and white porcelain is another repeated reference, long associated with the Ming Dynasty, which had a huge export trade in porcelain with Europe in the seventeenth and eighteenth centuries. The porcelains, including the patterns, were then adapted by the Europeans, and re-adapted by the Chinese, the willow pattern being among the most desired.

The voluptuous peach with its rosy bloom, believed to be native to China, can be likened in form to breasts, buttocks, and a heart—and, surprisingly, the shape of *Angry Birds*. A symbol of immortality and fertility in many Eastern mythologies, the peach also wards off evil. Moon uses the shape often, a nod to her home state of Georgia, known as the peach state.

Other motifs such as dragons, tigers, lanterns, and pagodas appear in Moon's lexicon in the guise of mass-produced kitsch and facile stereotypes but also as the residue of a revered tradition long abandoned by most contemporary Asian artists. They are as keenly aware of international trends and as engaged by current issues at home and abroad as their peers around the world, part of a millennial generation with little inclination for nostalgia.

More provocative is her *Angry Bird* "gook" vase, a derogatory term once freely applied to Asians (originally used by U.S. troops in Korea and Vietnam) without distinguishing among its vastly different countries and cultures, which cannot be meaningfully lumped together. Scrawled in black across a prettily glazed rosy pot, its demureness makes the word both more shocking and less so—the effect a muddling of intention, the barb muffled—or not. There is also a trend of late by those mocked to re-possess what was considered derisive as badges of honor.

The letter F that appears on a ceramic plaque brings to mind the start of an Anglo-Saxon expletive that has become rather innocuous due to overuse, but still not printable or utterable in certain media and situations. Moon slyly places the letter U, in case we missed the point, a bit away from it. However, she gives an extra twist to the linkage since her U is also a horseshoe, a symbol of good luck. Adding another layer of meaning to it: if the letters are combined, they are a transliteration of the Chinese character "fu," which also means luck, a character that appears in Korean and Japanese, both languages using a native script as well as one based on Chinese ideograms. Moon's sweet, sour, and spicy show is full of these fortuitous connections that viewers can interpret according to their own unpredictable associations, a whimsical interaction that is another of her work's great attractions.

Constructing an installation that sums up her themes, Moon assembles an ironic mélange of an East Asian interior with low, carved wooden tables placed on tatami mats and a few silk cushions scattered about. On the tables are vases with plants and miscellaneous, tchotchke-like pottery, as if set for her own version of a mad tea party. Floated on the sense and nonsense of cultural conventions and hierarchies, slippery, shape-shifting identities and the miracle of human variability and similarities, Moon's eclectic, idiosyncratic venture is both serious and fun, her embrace of the disparate exhilarating. A journey of sorts, like Alice's, Moon's art brings us a dazzling array of information, ideas, and images that in the ungrammatical words of her fictional counterpart, becomes wondrously "curiouser and curiouser."

Left:
Farmer's Song
2010
ink and acrylic, fabric on Hanji mounted on panel
18 x 18"
Courtesy of the artist and Curator's Office

Right:
Big Pennsylvania Dutch Korean Painting
2011
ink and acrylic, fabric, stickers, embroidery patches on Hanji
57 x 64"
Courtesy of the artist

Bat Bok
2010
ink and acrylic, fabric on Hanji mounted on panel
21 ½ x 30 ½"
Courtesy of Ryan Lee Gallery LLC

Far Left:
Double Bless
2012
ink and acrylic on Hanji, shoelaces, doily, pony beads, quilted border
41 x 16 ¾"
Courtesy of the artist

Left:
Detour
2012
ink and acrylic, fabric, Hanji, embroidery patches on Hanji, quilted border
40 ¼ x 30"
Courtesy of the artist

Right:
Yellow Dust
2012
ink and acrylic, spray paint, sticker on Hanji
36 ¾ x 25"
Courtesy of the artist

Day for Night 2
2012
ink and acrylic, glitter on Hanji mounted on panel
24 x 34"
Courtesy of the artist

Left:
Peach Mask II
2013
ink and acrylic on Hanji
38 x 38 ½"
Courtesy of the artist

Right:
Lucky Smile
2013
ink and acrylic, fabric and embroidery patches on Hanji
36 x 40 ½"
Courtesy of Ryan Lee Gallery LLC

Left:
Forever Couplehood
2014
ink and acrylic, screen print on Hanji
36 x 25 ½"
Courtesy of the artist

Right:
The Story I Did Not Know About
2014
ink and acrylic on Hanji
36 x 25 ½"
Courtesy of the artist

Left:
Peach Mask IV (LOVE)
2014
ink and acrylic, tie-dye cotton fabric on Hanji
40.5 x 38 ½"
Courtesy of Ryan Lee Gallery LLC

Right:
Peach Mask V (Foreign Love)
2014
ink and acrylic, gold leaf on Hanji
35 x 32 ½"
Courtesy of the artist

Left:
Double Welcome
2014
ink and acrylic on Hanji mounted on canvas
18 x 18"
Courtesy of Ryan Lee Gallery LLC

Right:
Blue Willow Slope
2014
ink and acrylic on Hanji mounted on canvas
24 x 20"
Courtesy of Ryan Lee Gallery LLC

Left:
Letter Shin (Yellow)
2014
cyanotype, ink and acrylic, rhinestones on paper
25 x 25"
Courtesy of the artist

Right:
Letter Shin (White)
2015
cyanotype, ink and acrylic, doily on paper
19 x 19"
Courtesy of the artist

Familiar Faces
2015
ink and acrylic on Hanji mounted on canvas
28 x 44"
Courtesy of the artist and Curator's Office

Left:
Like
2015
ink and acrylic, nail decal on Hanji
58 x 42"
Courtesy of the artist and Mindy Solomon Gallery

Right:
Double Double
2015
ink and acrylic on Hanji, fabric, quilted border
56.5 x 30 ½"
Courtesy of the artist

Most Everyone's Mad Here
2015
ink and acrylic on Hanji mounted on canvas
28 x 44"
Courtesy of the artist

Left:
Myo I (Day)
2016
cyanotype, ink and acrylic, rhinestones on paper
15 x 15"
Courtesy of the artist and Reynolds Gallery

Right:
Myo II (Night)
2014
cyanotype, ink and acrylic on paper
16 x 16"
Courtesy of the artist and Reynolds Gallery

Left:
Letter Shin (Gold)
2016
cyanotype, ink and acrylic, nail decal on paper
19 x 19"
Courtesy of the artist

Right:
Letter Shin: Blue Willow
2015
cyanotype, ink and acrylic on paper
20 x 18"
Courtesy of the artist

Hello Monkey
2013
ceramic, hand-knotted synthetic
hair, pony beads, found objects,
thread
46 x 9 ¾ x 2"
Courtesy of the artist

New Bride
2013
ceramic, hand-knotted synthetic
hair, pony beads, thread
28 x 5 x 2 ¼"
Courtesy of the artist

Harley Crow
2013
ceramic, hand-knotted synthetic
hair, wooden beads, found objects
28 x 5 x 2 ¼"
Courtesy of Ryan Lee Gallery LLC

Marie
2013
ceramic, hand-knotted synthetic
hair, Hanji beads, wooden beads,
thread, wire
32 x 6 x 1 ½"
Courtesy of the artist

Gloria
2013
ceramic, hand-knotted synthetic
hair, acrylic paint, found object
27 x 5 x 1 ½"
Courtesy of Ryan Lee Gallery LLC

Hosoon
2013
ceramic, hand-knotted synthetic hair, pony beads, shells, thread, wire
33 x 8 ¼ x 1 ¼"
Courtesy of the artist

Bette
2013
ceramic, hand-knotted synthetic hair, Hanji, wire
28 x 3 ¾ x 1"
Courtesy of the artist

Wise Nell
2013
ceramic, hand-knotted synthetic hair, beads, thread
21 x 4 x 2"
Courtesy of Ryan Lee Gallery LLC

Sandra
2013
ceramic, hand-knotted synthetic hair, wooden beads, Hanji beads, pony beads, found objects, thread
30 x 3 ½ x 1"
Courtesy of Ryan Lee Gallery LLC

Andrea
2013
ceramic, hand-knotted synthetic hair, pony beads, thread, found objects
34 x 4 x 1"
Courtesy of the artist

White Tiger
2014
ceramic, hand-knotted synthetic
hair, found objects, beads, plastic
hair barrettes, wire
33 x 7 x 2"
Courtesy of the artist

Owl Lady
2014
ceramic, hand-knotted synthetic
hair, plastic beads, found objects,
shoelaces, wire
33 x 5 x 2 ½"
Courtesy of the artist

Blue Maria
2014
ceramic, hand-knotted synthetic
hair, pony and plastic beads, found
objects, wire
26 x 6 x 3"
Courtesy of the artist

Masa
2014
ceramic, hand-knotted synthetic
hair, shoelaces, wooden chopstick,
wire
38 x 10 x 2 ½"
Courtesy of the artist

Rachel
2014
ceramic, hand-knotted synthetic
hair, human hair, plastic barrettes,
wool, found objects, wire
27 x 6 x 3"
Courtesy of the artist

Double Ginger
2014
ceramic, hand-knotted synthetic hair, found objects, Hanji beads, shoelaces, leather, wire
28 x 8 x 2"
Courtesy of the artist

Moonface
2015
ceramic, hand-knotted synthetic hair, found objects, wire
33 x 6 ½ x 2"
Courtesy of the artist

Lahr
2014
ceramic, hand-knotted synthetic hair, found objects, plastic beads, wire
33 x 6 x 2 ½"
Courtesy of the artist

Blue Bird
2014
ceramic, hand-knotted synthetic hair, feathers, fabric, wooden beads, found objects
28 x 5 x 2 ½"
Courtesy of the artist

Lucky
2013
ceramic, hand-knotted and braided synthetic hair, pony beads, ceramic beads
30 x 8 x 2"
Courtesy of the artist

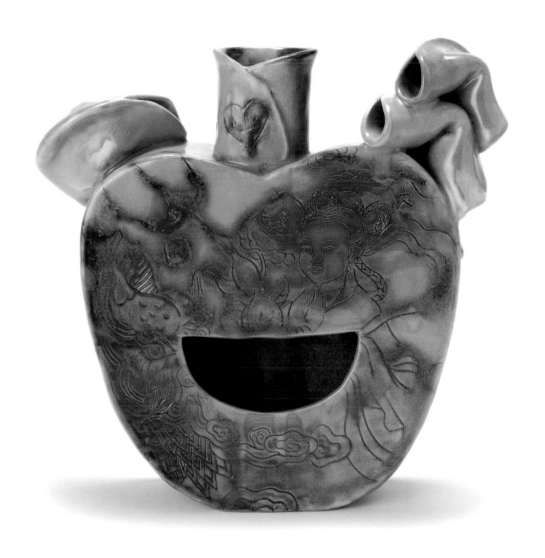

Left:
Lady Fortune Heart Vase
2013
earthenware ceramic
9 x 8.5 x 3 ½"
Collection of Diane and Garey De Angelis

Right:
La Sirena
2013
earthenware ceramic
8 x 9 ½ x 5"
Courtesy of the artist

Left:
Mutt
2013
earthenware ceramic
18.5 x 19 ½ x 3 ½"
Courtesy of the artist

Right:
Monkey
2013
earthenware ceramic
12 x 10 x 15"
Collection of Ann Huebner

Hipster Mustache Blue Willow & Fortune Cookies
2014
earthenware ceramic
10 ½ x 11 x 4 ½"
Courtesy of the artist

Angry Peach
2014
earthenware ceramic
5 x 4 ½ x 5"
Courtesy of the artist

Left:
Peach Eater
2014
earthenware ceramic
9 x 12 ½ x 9"
Courtesy of the artist

Right:
Mexican Korean Blue Willow Face Jug
2014
earthenware ceramic
6 x 5 x 5"
Courtesy of the artist

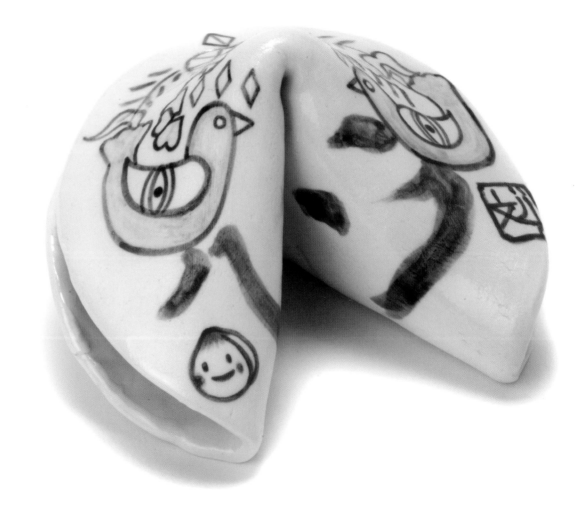

Left:
Double Fortune Cookie, Storyteller, Fortune Cookie #9
2014
earthenware, glaze, underglaze
4 x 4 x 4"
Courtesy of the artist

Right:
Fortune Cookie, Sim, Fortune Cookie #2
2014
porcelain, glaze, underglaze
4 x 4 x 3 ½"
Courtesy of the artist

Left:
Dragon, Fortune Cookie #5
2014
porcelain, glaze, underglaze
2 ½ x 4 x 2"
Courtesy of the artist

Right:
Lucky Jaguar, Fortune Cookie #8
2015
earthenware, glaze, underglaze
3.5 x 3 ½ x 3"
Courtesy of the artist

Left:
Youandl 3 (Blond)
2015
porcelain
3.5 x 4 ¼ x 4"
Courtesy of the artist

Right:
Lucky Face
2015
porcelain glaze, underglaze
4 x 4 x 3 ½"
Courtesy of the artist

Left:
Red Tiger
2015
earthenware glaze
9 x 8 x 7 ½"
Courtesy of the artist and Curator's Office

Right:
Yellow Chrysanthemum Gook
2015
earthenware, underglaze, glaze, hand-knotted synthetic hair
11 x 11 x 14 ½"

Left:
Ganesha Persica
2015
porcelain, earthenware, underglaze, glaze, hand-knotted
and braided synthetic hair
11.5 x 11 x 8 ½"
Courtesy of the artist

Right:
YOLO
2015
porcelain, underglaze, glaze, hand-knotted and braided
synthetic hair
7.5 x 8 x 12 ½"
Courtesy of the artist

Immortal Desert II (three views)
2015
porcelain, underglaze, glaze
15 x 14 x 10"
Courtesy of the artist and Mindy Solomon Gallery

Left:
Youandl 3 (Angry Peach)
2015
porcelain, underglaze, glaze, braided synthetic hair, plastic beads
5 x 20 x 4"
Courtesy of the artist

Right:
Anang
2015
earthenware, underglaze, glaze, braided synthetic hair, plastic barrette, wire
12 x 25 x 4 ½"
Courtesy of the artist

Left:
Maya
2015
earthenware, underglaze, glaze, braided synthetic hair, pony beads, wire
25 x 19 x 3 ½"
Courtesy of the artist

Right:
Horang
2015
earthenware, underglaze, glaze, synthetic hair, feather, wool,
shoelace, fabric, plastic chopstick
37 x 10 x 3"
Courtesy of the artist and Curator's Office

Far Right:
Baba
2015
earthenware, wire, hand-knotted synthetic hair, digitally printed fortune
cookie sayings, leather, metal bells, Hanji beads, beads
23 x 10 x 2 ½"
Courtesy of the artist and Curator's Office

Jiha Moon in conversation with Rachel Reese

Rachel Reese: Something I keep thinking of starting with is talking about your constant absorption of images and imagery in life, and how these ubiquitous signs and symbols creep into your practice. I was thinking it might be fun to talk about an "average" day for Jiha, and how and when your artistic practice blends with everyday routine.

Jiha Moon: I think that we are exposed to a flood of images and information even more now, since most everyone has a cell phone and an iPad; tablets and computers are everywhere. In one's device, those icons and symbols [provide] easy access for people to get into a different world by clicking on them. Visual images allow for a level of quick comprehension but also can be misunderstood or misleading. I am interested in this area of miscommunication in my work. Since we use our cell phones obsessively and daily, I think about that a lot.

But my everyday routine is simple. I work around my family's schedule and my studio practice, and within those two I juggle a lot. One often has to yield for others and I have to work with a flexible mind. I also work at night after my family goes to bed and that's when all the fun happens in my studio. It is my working habit. I am such a night owl and I work well at night. I often stay up pretty late …

RR: I love thinking about the word *archetype* in reference to your visual lexicon. Archetypes, versus stereotypes. When and how do you make the distinction?

JM: I am not sure if I draw a clear line between them but I definitely use those to play with peoples' minds. For example, I use Google typography to write [the word] Gook. People are already familiar with that style of typography and naturally accept it before they even read what's really written. I also place Twitter birds as a coupled image [in the] Pennsylvania Dutch folk-art style. I also draw peaches like body parts and Cupid doll cartoons all together in the same painting. Angry birds become peaches and smiley faces and Cupid dolls. They don't stay with their original identity but keep on changing into something else. These lexicons in my work are in flux.

RR: What drew you into the tactile world of clay and incorporating this medium into your practice? How long ago would you say it entered your practice, and do you remember the initial impulse?

JM: I have always loved making things with my hands and anything crafty. I used to watch my mother and my grandmother make household objects growing up, such as Korean blankets, which they would wash and sew just to change the cover sheets regularly instead of buying premade ones at the store. My grandmother always makes humble things to decorate her place and share with us. She would never call herself an artist or a quilter, but as a kid I saw these things around the house all the time and learned to love that aesthetic. I feel that this influenced me hugely today in my work.

As for how I entered clay world, I have always had the desire to make art objects. I feel that objects are something

friendly. Sometimes, I have a hard time thinking of making paintings this way. I call painting my cocky "boyfriend" as it is usually on the white wall in the white cube gallery space, and it can be often introduced to people in an unfriendly way. On the contrary, objects are sweet. Everyone has objects around in their place. People use them, collect them, and look at them. I have wanted to make art objects that are based on everyday objects that carry those personal feelings and stories. When I thought about that idea, ceramics were the perfect vehicle. So, I make these ceramic sculptures and think they could be helpful for people to get into my painting as well.

I have a minor in sculpture from graduate school but I think I got into ceramics more when I had a chance to go to a community clay studio. I could afford to pay for a membership from MOCA GA [Museum of Contemporary Art of Georgia] working on an artist fellowship in Atlanta in 2012. I mostly hand built stuff and I could get help from my assistant who threw for me at that time [2012–13]. After doing hand-building for several years, I felt that it was time to learn to throw on the wheel.

RR: I love the story about watching your mother and grandmother make objects by hand! Would you say you were raised in a traditional Korean household? Can you talk about your childhood in Korea? Do you feel your memories of home are most defined by specific moments or memories, or rather a more generalized sensibility?

JM: I feel both ways. Our family is in between a modern and traditional family. I grew up in Daegu, the third-largest city in South Korea, and it is pretty urban. I was there until high school. Then, I went to college and grad school in Seoul. I have to admit that my shock upon arrival in Seoul from my hometown as teenager was way bigger than arriving in America from Korea later on. Ha ha! Anyway, in my family, the kitchen was the women's hangout place as well as the working place where all the magical things happened. I grew up watching my mother, my two grandmothers, and often my aunts come to collaborate for a winter kimchi-making event that actually spread throughout our whole place. The entire house smelled like sesame oil and garlic. Eating culture has always been important to the family dynamic in Korea and people like to share food all the time.

RR: Can you remember and describe your memories of first moving to the United States?

JM: Yes, I remember my very first sensations when I arrived in Baltimore (in the fall of 1999), looking out the window and seeing all those trees and sky and thinking, Wow, this is the reason [American] people painted that way…. I was thinking about all those images that I have seen in art-history classes or books on Western art. Now, I feel the same way when I go back to Korea. Nature and environment are a big part of art.

And of course, I realized the minute I stepped in the country that my English sucked badly. Even after so many years of studying English in Korea, it did not matter.

RR: Can you tell me a story about how a familiar-yet-

foreign feeling, which affects your aesthetics and visual language so strongly, blends with your daily life? I keep thinking about the theory of the *umwelt*, which is essentially the idea that each individual (or organism, as in biology) carries a subjective and ever-evolving sense of normalcy with them in order to interpret and experience the world. I feel as if your *umwelt* is uncanny at its core. Does that make sense? I guess what I'm asking is, If you suddenly found yourself feeling complacent, would you seek out unease? How have you negotiated this?

JM: I definitely feel the sense of un-belonging and [of being] displaced often. [Having been] an artist for a long time, I realize that I am not all that social in other worlds, such as parents meetings at my kid's school, or taking my son to a new learning program after school for example. I feel that I am not so capable of doing things [other than art] and get overwhelmed easily. I often think, What am I ever good at? Making things in my studio is the easiest, I suppose, but that is NOT true either! It feels strange to prepare American-style meals that my family (my son and husband) would like to eat.

When I go to the community-based pottery studio, I often feel strange working in that environment. Even being in a Korean community in America makes me feel uneasy! All these activities make me feel uneasy sometimes, but then I accept that as my normal life: being uncomfortable or awkward. What is normal anyway? Is there any standard life that is supposed to be normal? I am not sure. If [a normal life did exist], I [would] probably feel pretty bored. Being in this constant stimulated situation [became a] given once I chose to be an artist, a Mom living in a foreign country as my adopted home. This is my normal, I guess. I try to make sense of it when I make work, and all of these [aspects of my life] are my sources of inspiration. In fact, I often like to channel these issues with a sense of humor in my work.

RR: Yes, I definitely see the unease re-channeled as humor, and to great effect. You essentially play with us as viewers, but we are made to believe we're in on the joke. The Czech novelist Milan Kundera made a famous observation that kitsch, and ultimately all sentimentality, redirects emotion from the object to the subject, which creates a fantasy of emotion without the real cost of feeling it. The kitsch object then encourages one to think, "Look at me looking at this thing," rather than, "I'm looking at this thing," in and of itself.

I once read of the term "pre-emptive kitsch," and I wonder if there is a layer to that in your work. You are using signs and symbols of kitsch from various contexts and cultures and consciously claiming and critiquing them. Are you out-kitsching the kitsch through this reflexive dialog? Perhaps this is ultimately a question of artistic pretenses and intent.

JM: I *love* how you say "out-kitsching the kitsch"! Yes, and ironically I want to believe that I can create some sort of emotion by "out-kitsching the kitsch"! Like I mentioned earlier, the meaning of these iconic images are not staying where they have originated. Not only just these iconic images, but I also consider other artifacts or even colors in this way. When I use Korean rainbow-colored stripes, tie-dye colors, fortune cookies, they all have their original stories yet have cultural misunderstandings at the same time. What about "fortune cookies"? They are all kitschy to begin with! It's the same with the blue willow pattern; its original idea was a cliché.

I like to put something classy and something cheesy on the same page for that reason. You can interpret that combination as something traditional and something more pop culture, or something old and something new. These iconic images often get distorted, shifted from their original images, and they interact with their environments (colors and space) to create a drama. Hopefully, that drama causes some emotions ... something funny, ridiculous, confused, sad, or happy would be great.

RR: Would you say that your practice is more appropriately

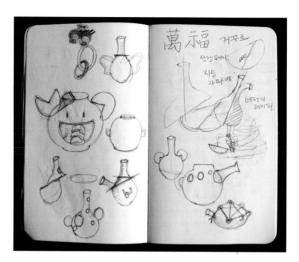

So, even if I start out with a simple idea, my work tends to evolve with many ideas at the end, and sometimes it goes in a completely different direction. The first idea is always as starting point but never the goal. I usually allow different ideas to interrupt my original ideas and see if I can make a better work. I am interested in creating new meanings in my work. Perhaps that means I confuse the viewers sometimes. Meanings are tricky. Meanings don't define images or give clear answers in my work, I hope. One image that defines one meaning is boring and not exciting to me. I try to avoid easy symbolism. I ask those symbols and signs to act in response to their environment in my work.

I believe in complexity. Every person I meet is a complex human being despite the fact that they have [different] ethnicities, genders, ages, backgrounds, eye and hair colors, lifestyles, education, and tastes. We often miss the individual's unique quality because of these labels. Misunderstandings can happen because of these given facts. I try to show that by combining, switching, changing, and misplacing visual elements with colors, patterns, repetitions, and juxtapositions, and by appropriating popular symbols.

RR: Do you think your age affects the way you absorb and interpret symbols and visual languages any more or less so than your identity as a Korean American does? I know this sounds funny, but I find myself on the cusp of two different generations: I'm what has been dubbed as the "Oregon Trail Generation" on social media—too old to feel like a Millennial, too young to be a Generation Xer. This definitely describes me! And it certainly affects the way I behave with

approached as a gestalt, rather than through individual ideas, components, or even individual artworks? Or, perhaps alternatively, are you more interested in a personal semiotic language that develops from your practice—signs and symbols that communicate meaning through repetition, patterns, appropriations, juxtapositions?

JM: Gestalt? I like that word! For almost all my work I balance between spontaneity and planned-out images during my process. I never just follow the one direction and complete [the work]. Just as much as I paint or build, I try to see what I have done in each step. I watch my acts and tendencies to see if I can develop them to an exciting stage.

technology and the Internet—half analogue, half digital. You are ten years older than I am, so I wonder if this is something you think about, and how it affects your engagement with digital platforms and therefore the images you absorb and use, like social media brand marks, the Angry Birds characters, Disney characters, etc. And again, how your identity as a Korean living in America comes into play.

JM: Yes, I think about this very often! I am a Generation Xer, and when we were young we were treated like some kind of punks. Now Gen Xers are in their late thirties and forties. Once upon a time, we were punks! I am watching and observing all the time. I say that I am like a SpongeBob [Squarepants] who just sucks all the info and makes it into the work! Of course, there are Gen X and Korean American perspectives in my work if you closely analyze it. I use certain social media brand marks and characters in my work like actors. You see, those images, logos, emojis are also changing, and as they get older new designs come out. So, that could relate to my specific works. I am happy with that. It is fun to imagine Millennials looking at my work through their cell phones and tablets and zooming in and out to see the details and finding these things and saying, "Well, that Twitter bird logo is old!" And one day they [might] see my work in person and talk about this topic … [it] would be great. Technology has certainly changed how people view art nowadays. I will continuously observe and reflect that in my artwork. That's how I respond to the world as an artist.

RR: Yes, and it's wild to think of the simulacrum of viewing art objects only on a screen, and never in person.

JM: Well, that actually drives me crazy. I once saw some young Korean celebrity talking that way on TV, saying he doesn't understand why he has to go to a museum when he is traveling because he can see all that stuff on his smartphone! Duh! But hopefully, someday he happens to see some amazing work of art in person that will change his mind. I don't ignore him. He represents a group from a

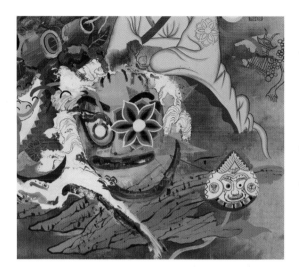

RR: Where and how are you in a debate over tradition? Do you find the need to wrestle with tradition to move forward and make something new? And to this point, how do you think representations of Korean and American values, histories, and culture change over time? I imagine your headspace is in constant battle between high and low, fine craft and kitsch, analogue communication and digital technology; you seem to thrive in these oppositional contexts.

JM: I am constantly looking and obsessed with old beauties here and there. Honestly, to find these traditions I use the Internet and actually that becomes handy. I find museum info, books, and catalogues through online archives from museums here and in Korea. I am sure many artists do the same. Something that digital media cannot satisfy for me is my very own visual experiences. So finding this inspiration is always exciting and new to me. I also see tremendous metaphors in tradition that speaks well in the contemporary world. I see this as the possibility of co-existing or collaborating rather than battling between two opposites: past and present. And about making something new?! I give up. Ha ha! I can only try to show my new perspective of seeing things through my work.

younger generation, and art somehow has to communicate with these youngsters, too.

Well, I love traditional beauty just as much as I love popular cultures. I believe there is a certain permanent beauty in classical work. I feel that when I visit museums and stand in front of old master works like Fra Angelico's or Rembrandt's paintings! This does not ever come across looking at images online.

I often use stained brown Hanji because the color and texture of this handmade mulberry paper reminds me of old book pages, or sepia drawings or etchings from the European Renaissance period. So, I try to think of aging as something beautiful ... becoming part of history.

RR: While I can certainly see the Eastern aesthetic influences and your playful appropriation of them in your work, I wonder about any Western aesthetic influences, in that, are there truly any Western aesthetics? What do you think about this and how do you want this conversation to be discussed in your practice? What I wonder is, can we really prescribe a nationalist Western (presumably American) aesthetic value to images like the Disney characters or social media icons when they are so globally disseminated now? Perhaps in the 1950s when Disney was so distinctly American, but now, in 2016? So then I start to wonder about the balance between stereotypes that you employ: the Eastern tropes versus Western or global tropes. What do you think?

JM: Before we talk about my Eastern/Western influences, I [want to say I] think my work is extremely individualistic. Haha! Tao Chi [late seventeenth–early eighteenth-century Taoist painter] called himself that when people liked to talk too much about his work based on influences or schools. I want to point out that my paintings are heavily camouflaged and layered. Obvious references are often hidden or twisted. Also, you can't really pinpoint where some elements come from. Some people will see certain of my works as in a typical Asian style—for example, Big Pennsylvania Dutch Korean Painting—but it actually is based on Pennsylvania Dutch folk art and hex signs. The birds are not mandarin ducks but goldfinches. So, that painting is influenced by American/Western folk art but it looks ridiculously Asian-like to many people. What can you say?

I use acrylic paint (which is a very young American material) to paint on Korean Hanji (an old, traditional mulberry paper). And my new adventure is to draw and paint on ceramic surfaces; that is my new playground! You know, ceramic has a long history of exchange between East and West. Honestly though, when I work in my studio I easily let myself get lost and often forget all about an Eastern/Western type of thinking and just make work.

I guess I am curious if anyone can define what style or "ism" can be perceived as distinctively American art? America is such a melting pot, embracing all types of people from other countries and their cultures in one nation. It is hard to define a singular way to describe an American national style. I am in awe of abstract expressionism and pop art from the 1960s but also I…appreciate contemporary American art, which has more diverse artists, including female artists, in it, but I do not necessarily think that I am influenced by American art. I love all types of folk art, women's quilts and embroidery work, designs, minority art in America. I often find these in tourist places or little towns in America, and, surprisingly, I found out that [many folk art traditions] are adopted from elsewhere! The world is so interconnected these days, and geographical distinctions do not matter much.

RR: I must admit that yes, this question alone indicates how American I am. I think the exact same could be said for, "Is there really a distinct Eastern aesthetic?" as in, we likewise project stereotypes.

JM: Yes, my biggest Asian influences are often from Korea's neighboring countries, China and Japan. There are a lot of common aesthetics among the three countries, to be honest, and I don't expect people, especially Westerners, to distinguish the details. And I don't get offended by that.

On the other hand, this is ridiculous but I still get questions from people such as, "Why are you making fortune cookies? You are Korean, not Chinese!"

RR: Can you talk about your role as a storyteller and how, or even if, you identify with Korean storytelling as an art form? While your stories are visual rather than oral (and while the choice to travel is your own), the feeling of movement, travel, and perhaps a subsequent muddying of cultural contexts remains a crucial schema in your work. I think of the ancient Korean *Hwarang*, or *pansori* singers (a famous oral tradition of telling children stories in Korea), and wonder if any of this nationalist storytelling history plays a role in your aesthetic decisions, especially when considering adornment and decoration in your work, in particular the norigae sculptures.

JM: I love *pansori* and other traditional art forms from Korea. As a child I always wished that I had some sort of talent for singing or dancing, but no. Luckily, my sister is the one who has it (she is a dancer). I've looked for those for my own interests. Too funny there is this *pansori* story called "BulJubuJeon," with a hare and a tortoise, although it is entirely different from Western one having the same animals as main characters. Of course, I had to use this when I made art! In the pansori version, the hare is the winner, the smart one. He rides on the turtle's back to travel into the deep ocean and saves his own life when he recognizes the turtle's lie. I have made some iconic images based on Korean stories and folk art. In *Forever Couplehood* I used

screen printing and hand coloring, and I added an "F" logo from social media, highlighting two entirely opposite stories from East and West in my work.

For the *norigae* work I looked at a lot of folk [objects, including] Korean Tal and Hopi kachina dolls, African and Mexican masks, emojis, and ugly-face jugs from the [American] South. Many of these masks are [used in] performances that portray certain characters as satirical and humorous. When I first started this project I wanted to make the [*norigae* pieces] more like people, kind of creating portraits with my imagination, or I wanted to make objects that carried the kind of personality or characters that I saw in books or movies. I have also looked at how people wear their hair. I've learned to do dreadlocks and fishtail and different types of hairstyles by watching YouTube tutorials; [I use them] along with Korean traditional knots. Basically, I want these guys to remind people of all kinds of people. People carry lots of stories and people are the inspiration for these *norigae*.

RR: The word foreign is used a lot in reference to your practice, both as a term to describe something "other" and in opposition to what is "familiar," but I also wonder if foreign becomes almost blanket terminology to allow for dismissive stereotypes or lazy categorizations with reference to something that is simply strange and new. Is there a distinction for you? Do you identify with an emotional or conceptual connection to the word?

JM: When I had a show at the Museum of Contemporay Art of Georgia in Atlanta in 2013, I titled my show *Foreign Love.* It also sounds like "fall in love," and I like to point out that people tend to fall in love with foreign stuff when they travel around.... People love something unfamiliar and add on to it in their imaginations [so they can] think of it as authentic or exotic. I see how people do that in my practice as well, though [this is] not always positive, and I do get people who make easy assumptions about my work; as you just said, they "stereotype" my work. They see the work on the surface level and define it as Asian art. It is a lazy categorization to see my work only in that way. I often have to point out my work is just as much American influenced as Korean influenced. So the word *foreign* is my reminder for people to think about what authenticity really means to them. Ultimately, everyone—except ourselves—is foreign to us. I think examining misunderstanding is part of the necessary process of understanding others.

Rachel Reese is *Associate Curator of Modern and Contemporary Art at Telfair Museums in Savannah, Georgia.*

Selected Chronology

Born Daegu, South Korea
Lives and works in Atlanta, Georgia

EDUCATION
2002   M.F.A., University of Iowa, School of Art and Art History, Iowa City
2001   M.A., University of Iowa, School of Art and Art History, Iowa City
1999   M.F.A., Ewha University, Seoul, South Korea
1996   B.F.A., Korea University, Seoul, South Korea

SOLO EXHIBITIONS
2015   *Double Welcome: Most Everyone's Mad Here*, Halsey Institute of Contemporary Art, Charleston, South Carolina (catalogue); Taubman Museum, Roanoke, Virginia; Kalamazoo Institute of Arts, Kalamazoo, Michigan; Salina Art Center, Salina, Kansas; Jule Collins Smith Museum of Fine Art, Auburn, Alabama; Richard E. Peeler Art Center, Greencastle, Indiana; Tarble Arts Center, Charleston, Illinois; American University Art Museum, Washington, DC.
2014   *Foreign Love*, Weatherspoon Museum of Art, Greensboro, North Carolina.
        Foreign Love Too, Ryan Lee Gallery, New York, New York.
2013   *Foreign Love*, Museum of Contemporary Art of Georgia, Atlanta, Georgia.
        All Kinds of Everything, Savannah College of Art and Design, Savannah, Georgia, and Atlanta, Georgia.
2012   *Souvenir Valise*, Curator's Office, Washington, DC.
        Stars Down to Earth, James Gallery, CUNY Graduate Center, New York, New York.
        Detourist, Saltworks Gallery, Atlanta, Georgia.
        Springfield, Arario Gallery, Seoul, South Korea (catalogue).
2011   *Colliding Icon*, Cheekwood Botanical Garden and Museum, Nashville, Tennessee.
        Day for Night, Clough-Hanson Gallery, Rhode College, Memphis, Tennessee (catalogue).
        Chutes and Tears, The Lab, (Project exhibition with Rachel Hayes), New York, New York.
2010   *American Appendage*, Mary Ryan Gallery, New York, New York.
2010   *Blue Peony and Impure Thoughts*, Saltworks Gallery, Atlanta, Georgia.
2009   *An Exact Place*, Curator's Office, Washington, DC.
        Jiha Moon/Nate Moore: Recent Works, Roberts C. Williams Paper Museum, Atlanta, Georgia.
2008   *Vantage Point VII: Jiha Moon: Turbulent Utopia*, The Mint Museum, Charlotte, North Carolina (catalogue).
        Megaxiscape, Moti Hasson Gallery, New York, New York.

2008	*No Peach Heaven: MuRung Dowan*, Saltworks Gallery, Atlanta, Georgia (catalogue).
2007	*Line Tripping*, Curator's Office, Washington, DC (catalogue).
	Fabulous Fiction, Moti Hasson Gallery, New York, New York.
2007	*Stain Trivia: Take-out Drawing* [project exhibition], Seoul, South Korea.
2006	*Pleasant Purgatory*, Brain Factory, Seoul, South Korea (catalogue).
2005	*Symbioland*, Curator's Office, Washington, DC (catalogue).
2004	*New Work*, Greenbelt Art Center, Greenbelt, Maryland.
	New Work, Elizabeth Roberts Gallery, Washington, DC.
	Hypermeltedfictioncontradiction, Dega Gallery, Mclean, Virginia.
2003	*I'll Meet You There*, Korean Cultural Service, Washington, DC.
	Moonscape, Mclean Project for the Arts, Mclean, Virginia.
2002	*Absolute Narrative*, Eve Drewelowe Gallery, University of Iowa, Iowa City.

SELECTED GROUP EXHIBITIONS

2016	*Peachtree Industry*, Bodega, New York, New York.
	A Whisper of Where It Came From, Kemper Museum, Kansas City, Missouri.
2015	*Organic Matters*, National Museum of Women in the Arts, Washington, DC.
	Beauty Reigns, Akron Museum, Akron, Ohio.
2014	*The Lineage of Vision: Progress through Persistence*, Gallery Korea, Korean Cultural Service, New York, New York (catalogue).
	Past Traditions/New Voices in Asian Art, Hofstra University Museum, Hempstead, New York.
	Hunter Invitational III, Hunter Museum, Chattanooga, Tennessee.
	Beauty Reigns, McNay Museum, San Antonio, Texas.
	Ink & Paper, High Museum of Art, Atlanta, Georgia.
2013	*Drawing inside the Perimeter*, High Museum of Art, Atlanta, Georgia.
	Painterly Gesture, Columbus State University, Columbus, Georgia.
	showing/thinking, Dalton Gallery, Agnes Scott College, Atlanta, Georgia.
2012	Maier Museum, Randolph College, Lynchburg, Virginia.
2011	*New American Voices II*, Fabric Workshop and Museum, Philadelphia, Pennsylvania.
	85th Annual International Competition: Printmaking, The Print Center, Philadelphia, Pennsylvania.
	Movers and Shakers, The Museum of Contemporary Art of Georgia, Atlanta.

2010	*Recent Acquisitions*, Virginia Museum of Fine Art, Richmond, Virginia.
	Hudgens Prize Finalists Exhibition, Hudgens Center for the Art, Duluth, Georgia.
	Departures and Arrivals, Towson University, Baltimore, Maryland.
	New Faces, Andrew Bae Gallery, Chicago, Illinois.
	Women of the Year, Smith College Museum of Art, Northampton, Massachusetts.
2010–2009	*More Mergers and Acquisitions* [collaboration with Rachel Hayes], The Atlanta Contemporary Art Center, Atlanta, Georgia.
2009	*Between the Lines: Jiha Moon and Sungsoon Youm* [project exhibition], Project Space Sarubia, Seoul, South Korea.
	An Intricate Touch, Miki Wick Kim Contemporary, Zurich, Switzerland.
	5 Cubed: Multiplicity of Contemporary Art from South Korea, Mary Ryan Gallery, New York, New York.
2009–2008	*40th Anniversary Art on Paper 2008*, Weatherspoon Museum of Art, Greensboro, North Carolina (catalogue).
2008	*Currents: Recent Acquisitions*, Hirshhorn Museum and Sculpture Garden, Washington, DC.
	Movement, Smith College Museum of Art, Northampton, Massachusetts.
	New Prints 2008/Spring, International Print Center of New York, New York.
2008–2006	*One Way or Another: Asian American Art Now*, Asia Society and Museum, New York, New York (catalogue); Blaffer Art Museum, University of Houston, Texas; Berkeley Art Museum, University of California; Japanese American National Museum, Los Angeles.
2007	*Jiha Moon and Franklin Evans*, Miki Wick Kim Contemporary Art, Zurich, Switzerland.
	Talent Show: 2007 Atlanta Biennial, Atlanta Contemporary Art Center, Atlanta, Georgia.
	Levity, The Drawing Center, New York, New York (catalogue).
2007	*This Many*, Saltworks Gallery, Atlanta, Georgia.
2006	*Asia Society's 10 Artists Print Portfolio*, Asia Society and Museum, New York, New York.
	Asian Contemporary Art in Print, Singapore Tyler Print Institute, Singapore.
	The Real (Art) World: 5 Curators. 5 Artists. 1 Museum, American University Museum at the Katzen Arts Center, Washington, DC.
	Animalia, Irvine Contemporary, Washington DC.

2005 *Bethesda Trawick Prize Exhibition*, Creative Partners Gallery, Bethesda, Maryland.
Boundaries: Contemporary Landscape, Union Gallery, University of Maryland, College Park.
Red Beans and Rice, Atlanta Contemporary Art Center, Atlanta, Georgia.
Strictly Painting 5, Mclean Project for the Arts, Mclean, Virginia.
State of the Art: Mid-Atlantic Overview, Arlington Arts Center, Arlington, Virginia.
Family Sublime, Park School, Brooklandville, Maryland.

2004 *Semi-Lucid,* White Columns, New York, New York.
Technature, Kunstoffice, Berlin, Germany.
Storytellers, Los Medanos College Gallery, Pittsburg, California.

2003 *Världar Welten Worlds Saegae*, Atelierhaus Mengerzeile, Kunstalle m3, Berlin, Germany.
2003 *Hand and Eye* [Artists-in-Residence Exhibition], Wesley Seminary, Washington, DC.
2002 *Midwest Ticket*, Gallery 119, Chicago, Illinois.
2002 *M.F.A. Exhibition*, University of Iowa Museum of Art, Iowa City.
In Between, Byron Buford Gallery, University of Iowa, Iowa City.
Fully Integrated, Dega Gallery, McLean, Virginia.
Summer Salon, Ellipse Arts Center, Arlington, Virginia.

2001 *Small Paintings*, Byron Burford Gallery, University of Iowa, Iowa City.
Appendage, Eve Drewelowe Gallery, University of Iowa, Iowa City.

2000 *For Family*, Byron Burford Gallery, University of Iowa, Iowa City.
Funny Bones, Byron Burford Gallery, University of Iowa, Iowa City.

1999 *10 Plus 4*, Fox Building, Maryland Art Institute, Baltimore, Maryland.
Field, Gwan-Hoon Gallery, Seoul, South Korea.

SELECTED BIBLIOGRAPHY

Baker, Alex, juror. *New American Paintings: Juried Exhibitions in Print*. No. 63, Mid Atlantic (April/May 2006), https://newamericanpaintings.com/artists/jiha-moon.

Capps, Kriston. "Jiha Moon: Line Tripping." *Washington City Paper*, October 3, 2007, http://www.washingtoncitypaper.com/arts/article/13008606/jiha-moon-line-tripping.

Cash, Stephanie. "Jiha Moon's tae kwon do art ebulliently melds East, West, high and low." *ArtsATL*, September 17, 2013, http://www.artsatl.com/2013/09/review-jiha-moon-2/.

Cochran, Rebecca Dimling. *Art in America* (May 2008): 201.

Cohen, David. "Weather Channels: Christopher Cook at Mary Ryan Gallery, Richard Ballard at Robert Steele Gallery, Jiha Moon at Moti Hasson Gallery." *New York Sun*, May 17, 2007, http://www.nysun.com/arts/weather-channels/54710/.

Colvin, Rob. "In Survey of Southern Art, Place Is the Space." *Hyperallergic*, Sept. 5, 2014, http://hyperallergic.com/136334/in-survey-of-southern-art-place-is-the-space/.

"Critic's Pick, Atlanta: 'Jiha Moon at Saltworks.'" *Artforum* (February 2010), http://artforum.com/picks/id=24923.

Cudlin, Jeffry. "Symbioland." *Washington City Paper*, October 29, 2005, http://www.washingtoncitypaper.com/arts/article/13031889/symbioland.

Dawson, Jessica. "In Moon's Work, the Eyes Have It." *The Washington Post*, August 15, 2004, p. CO5.

Dawson, Jessica. "Jiha Moon's Fantasy Island." *The Washington Post*, September 15, 2005, p. C05.

Fallon, Roberta. "New American Voices: A 4-Course Art Feast." *Philadelphia Weekly*, February 16, 2011, http://philadelphiaweekly.com/2011/feb/16/emNew-American-Voicesem-a-4-Course-Art-Feast/#.V1CRKr5QDuA.

Feaster, Felicia. "Jiha Moon: Peach Pit." *Creative Loafing/Atlanta*, January 23, 2008. http://clatl.com/atlanta/jiha-moon-peach-pit/Content?oid=1271722.

Feaster, Felicia. "Visual overload fuels 'Foreign Love,'" *The Atlanta Journal-Constitution*, September 12, 2013, http://www.myajc.com/news/entertainment/visual-overload-fuels-foreign-love/nZq8w/.

Fox, Catherine. *The Atlanta Journal-Constitution*, Friday, February 12, 2010, p.D12.

Fox, Catherine. "Jiha Moon as ebullient, bemused, observant 'tourist' in sumptuous show at Saltworks." ArtsATL, May 3, 2012, http://www.artsatl.com/author/cathy/page/29/.

Howell, George. *Art Papers* (January/February 2006): 71.

Hutson, Laura. "By mashing up common cultural touchstones, South Korean–born artist Jiha Moon explores our national psyche." *Nashville Scene*, May 19, 2011, http://www.nashvillescene.com/nashville/by-mashing-up-common-cultural-touchstones-south-korean-born-artist-jiha-moon-explores-our-national-psyche/Content?oid=2450381.

Johnson, Ken. "The Listings: Art: 'Semi-Lucid.'" *The New York Times*, October 8, 2004, http://query.nytimes.com/gst/fullpage.html?res=9405E1D9153BF93BA35753C1A9629C8B63.

Kim, Miki Wick. *Korean Contemporary Art*. New York and London: Prestel Publishing, 2012.

Koeppel, Frederic. "Ideas, images flow uninterrupted in Jiha Moon's 'Day for Night.'" *The Commercial Apppeal/Memphis*, September 15, 2011, http://www.commercialappeal.com/entertainment/art-review-ideas-images-flow-uninterrupted-in-jiha-moons-day-for-night-ep-388253314-324192671.html.

Kotik, Charlotta, juror. "Jiha Moon." *New American Paintings: Juried Exhibitions in Print*. No. 70, South (June/July 2007), https://newamericanpaintings.com/artists/jiha-moon.

Kunitz, Daniel. "Defying the Definitive." *New York Sun*, September 14, 2006, http://www.nysun.com/arts/defying-the-definitive/39699/.

Lampe, Lilly. "Foreign Love Too." *ArtAsiaPacific*, March 2014, http://artasiapacific.com/Magazine/WebExclusives/ForeignLoveTooJihaMoon.

McClintock, Diana. *Art Papers* (March/April 2008): 53.

Oppenheim, Pill. "Talent Show, Atlanta." *Art Papers* (September/October 2007): 57.

O'Sullivan, Michael. "Jiha Moon's Shining Contrast." *The Washington Post*, September 16, 2005, p. WE57, http://www.washingtonpost.com/wpdyn/content/article/2005/09/15/AR2005091500574.html.

Pousner, Howard. "Moon pushes boundaries in MOCA GA exhibit 'Foreign Love,'" *The Atlanta Journal-Constitution*, September 4, 2013, http://www.myajc.com/news/entertainment/moon-pushes-boundaries-in-moca-ga-exhibit-foreign-/nZmjG/.

Rice, Robin. "Static Cling." *Philadelphia City Paper*, February 23, 2011.

Sirlin, Deanna. "Jiha Moon's candy coated chaos." *Creative Loafing/Atlanta*, February 7, 2010, http://clatl.com/atlanta/jiha-moons-candy-coated-chaos/Content?oid=1286691.

Smith, Roberta. "A Melange of Asian Roots and Shifting Identities." *New York Times*, September 8, 2006, http://www.nytimes.com/2006/09/08/arts/design/08asia.html?fta=y&_r=0.

Thornton, Grace. "Art Review: Jiha Moon's Detourist Exaggerates a Simplified View of Culture." *Burnaway*, April 25, 2012, http://burnaway.org/review/jiha-moons-detourist-exagerates-a-simplified-view-of-culture/.

Wei, Lilly. "Here's Looking at You." In *Beauty Reigns: A Baroque Sensibility in Recent Painting*. Exh cat. McNay Art Museum, 2014.

Wennerstrom, Nord. "Jiha Moon." *Artforum* (December 2007): 360.

Wolf, Deborah. "A colorful utopia melding cultures." *The Atlanta Journal-Constitution*, January 27, 2008.

Yang, Jeff. "Asian Pop/Art Breakers." *San Francisco Chronicle*, October 16, 2006, http://www.sfgate.com/entertainment/article/ASIAN-POP-Art-Breakers-3250330.php.a

Yau, John. "Kathy Butterly and the Aesthetic Challenge of 'No Two Alike.'" *Hyperallergic*, March 16, 2014, http://hyperallergic.com/113978/kathy-butterly-and-the-aesthetic-challenge-of-no-two-alike/.

Yau, John. "Postscript to the Whitney Biennial: An Asian American Perspective." *Hyperallergic*, June 29, 2014, http://hyperallergic.com/135205/postscript-to-the-whitney-biennial-an-asian-american-perspective/.

VISITING ARTIST

2016	Kemper Museum, Kansas City, Missouri
	Salina Art Center, Salina, Kansas
	Kalamazoo Institute of Art, Kalamazoo, Michigan
2015	University of Florida, Gainesville, Florida
	Columbus State University, Columbus, Georgia
2014	University of Colorado, Denver, Colorado
	University of Alabama, Tuscaloosa, Alabama
	Wofford College, Spartanburg, South Carolina
	Screen-print Workshop, Minnesota State University, Mankato, Minnesota
	Falk Visiting Artist, University of North Carolina, Greensboro, North Carolina
	McNay Museum, San Antonio, Texas
2013	Kirk Visiting Artist, Agnes Scott College, Atlanta, Georgia
	Savannah College of Arts and Design, Atlanta, Georgia
	Savannah College of Arts and Design, Savannah, Georgia
2012–2013	Artist in Residence, MOCA GA Working Artist Project, The Museum of Contemporary Art of Georgia, Atlanta, Georgia
2011	Montevallo University, Montevallo, Alabama
	Rhodes College, Memphis, Tennessee
2010	Artist in Residence, Landfall Press, Santa Fe, New Mexico
	Savannah College of Art and Design, Atlanta, Georgia
	Summer Blossom Visiting Artist, Kent University, Kent, Ohio
	American University, Washington, DC
	Screen-print Workshop, P.R.I.N.T., University of North Texas, Texas
	Smith College, Northampton, Massachusetts
2009–2010	Artist in Residence, Fabric Workshop and Museum, Philadelphia, Pennsylvania
2009	Artist in Residence, Acadia Summer Art Program, Bar Harbor, Maine
2008	Artist in Residence, Acadia Summer Art Program, Bar Harbor, Maine
	The Mint Museum, Charlotte, North Carolina
	Print Workshop, Flying Horse Editions, University of Central Florida, Florida
	Smith College Museum of Art, Northampton, Massachusetts

2007	Art Omi International Artists Residency, Ghent, New York
2006	Artist Residency at Singapore Tyler Print Institute, awarded by Asia Society and Museum, New York, New York
2005	American University, Washington, DC
2004	Artist in Residence, The Henry Luce III Center for the Arts and Religion, Washington, DC
	National Museum of Women in the Arts, Washington, DC
2003	Artist in Residence, Wesley Seminary, Washington, DC

GRANTS AND FELLOWSHIPS

2012-2013	Working artist project, The Museum of Contemporary Art of Georgia, Atlanta, GA
2011	The Joan Mitchell Foundation Painters & Sculptor's Grant Award, New York, New York
2010	Fellowship, The MacDowell Colony, Peterborough, New Hampshire
2008	Golden Foundation Fellowship, Headlands Center for the Arts, Sausalito, California
2005	The Trawick Prize, Bethesda Contemporary Art Awards, Bethesda, Maryland
2003	UCROSS Foundation, Clearmont, Wyoming
2002	Virginia Center for the Creative Arts, Sweet Briar, Virginia
2001–2002	Pelzer-Lynch Scholarship, School of Art and Art History, University of Iowa, Iowa City, Iowa
2000–2001	Lucida Mendenhalle Wile Scholarship, University of Iowa, Iowa City, Iowa
1993–1996	Korea University Scholarship, Korea University, Seoul, South Korea

SELECTED COLLECTIONS

Agnes Scott College, Atlanta, Georgia
Arario Gallery, Seoul, South Korea
Asia Society and Museum, New York, New York
Bank of America, Atlanta, Georgia
Citibank, New York, New York
District of Columbia City Hall Art Collection, Washington, DC
The Fabric Workshop and Museum, Philadelphia, Pennsylvania
High Museum of Art, Atlanta, Georgia
Hirshhorn Museum and Sculpture Garden, Smithsonian Institution, Washington, DC
Hunter Museum of American Art, Chattanooga, Tennessee
Microsoft Art Collection, New York, New York
Minnesota State University, Mankato, Minnesota
The Mint Museum, Charlotte, North Carolina
The Museum of Contemporary Art of Georgia, Atlanta, Georgia
National Museum of Women in the Arts, Washington, DC
Neuberger Berman Art Collection, New York, New York
OMI International Arts Center, Ghent, New York
Singapore Tyler Print Institute, Singapore
Smith College Museum of Art, Northampton, Massachusetts
UBS Art Collection, New York, New York
University of Central Florida, Orlando, Florida
University of Maryland, College Park, Maryland
Virginia Museum of Fine Arts, Richmond, Virginia
Weatherspoon Art Museum, University of North Carolina at Greensboro, Greensboro, North Carolina